MW01288524

Greg Hildenbrand

How Did I Miss That?

Spiritual Mysteries Hidden in Plain Sight

Greg Hildenbrand

Additional information, music, and resources are available at www.ContemplatingGrace.com.

ISBN: 1545287392
ISBN-13: 978-1545287392

Also by Greg Hildenbrand

Books:
Finding Grace in an Imperfect World
Finding Grace in Lent
Uncovering God in Christmas
Paul Wrote the Book of Love

Music CDs:
Finding Grace in an Imperfect World
Songs of Lent
Songs of Christmas

Ordering information at www.ContemplatingGrace.com

Dedication

I dedicate this book to an early, spiritual mentor, Larry Quade, who took a young man looking for answers and taught him that understanding is a journey, not a destination. This book documents part of what has been a long, strange, trip toward the shore that is no shore.

CONTENTS

Acknowledgements

Writing a book is always a group process, and this book is no exception. Special thanks to my lovely and talented daughter, Grace Marie, for her editing assistance. Thanks also to my friend and Saturday morning walking partner, Stan Hughes, for his insights, support, and recommendations for improvement. Finally, thank you to my wife, Carrie Ann, for allowing me the freedom to ponder the mysteries of life in a safe, loving, and supportive environment.

Introduction

I consider myself a reasonably intelligent person, but there is much I do not understand. Some of what is a mystery to me is simply beyond my intellectual ability to grasp. Some is hidden where I cannot find it. There is knowledge, however, that is neither hidden nor is it beyond my ability to grasp. It is here in plain view. I look directly upon it day after day, and I still miss it. I find there is a paradoxical facet to understanding that transcends intellect. Being able to reason an issue through is not necessarily the only or the best way of knowing. Before we can grasp a concept, we must be ready and willing to grasp it. Our minds must be sufficiently open to accept something new and different. In retrospect, once we grasp a paradoxical truth it seems as if we knew it all along, and we are simply *remembering*. We think, "How did I miss that?" Thus, the title of this book.

A Buddhist proverb reads, "When the student is ready, the teacher appears." I think the same is true of understanding. When we are ready to grasp a particular truth, our mind's eye will be opened to allow us to see it. Until that time, it is as if it does not exist. Sometimes, we must endure a life-altering event in order to be able to receive a new bit of wisdom that does not fit our previously held beliefs.

The following pages are full of truths that seem obvious to me now, although they were absent from my conscious understanding at other times in my life. I do not believe it was because I lacked intelligence, and it certainly was not that the knowledge was inaccessible to me. For whatever reason, my mind was not open enough to see it. *How Did I Miss That?* is a collection of reflections I first published as *Life Notes* on my website, www.ContemplatingGrace.com, in 2016 and early 2017.

Finally, a disclaimer. Those who write as if they understand something clearly and completely run the risk of misleading others, both about themselves and about their written material. I am far from all-knowing or infallible (as those who know me will readily attest). It is not my intent to pretend to know any final, universal, or comprehensive truth, although I may write as if I believe that to be the case. Rather, I am a seeker, like so many of my readers, and it is my hope that documenting my wrestling with less-than-obvious concepts will encourage others to engage in their own battle for understanding. What follows is a part of my journey. It is my hope and prayer that my journey will inspire you on yours and to remind you that you are in good company. In fact, I believe ours is the same journey experienced from two different points of reference. Perhaps you will find some of what you have missed in these pages, too. Regardless, the insights that follow have blessed me, and if they bless you in some small way, too, I am twice blessed.

Greg Hildenbrand
April 2017

1. The Bible is My Story

All scripture is inspired by God and is useful for teaching, for reproof, for correction, and for training in righteousness, so that everyone who belongs to God may be proficient, equipped for every good work. 2 Timothy 3:16-17

The Bible is difficult for me to read. It is hard to relate to, and harder yet to apply to my life. The violence that is sought and celebrated in the Old Testament troubles me, not to mention the apparent support for slavery, the lack of standing for women and children, and the over-the-top laws governing human behavior. Even the New Testament seems dated. I find myself justifying my casual attitude by saying it was written for another time, and times have changed. The problem, however, is not with the Bible, its authors, or the time in which it was written. The problem is that I have not recognized myself in its pages. I have always read it as someone else's story.

The first decades of my life were spent building my identity – who I am, what I do, and finding my place in the world. It has been about me, me, and me. This is a common and necessary focus for most of us early in our lives. I shared the life of Greg with others, of course – my wife and children, co-workers, and friends, but it was still *my* kingdom I was building, my *nation*, if you will. I dedicated significant energies to *winning*, even with the awareness that for me to win, others would lose. I believe the Old Testament can be read as the metaphorical story of the first half of our lives. The focus is on *nation-building*. It is full of win-lose scenarios. A nation is either the conqueror or the conquered, the persecutor or the persecuted, the slaveholder or the slave. I am not proud to confess that has been my story, too, constantly seeking to triumph over others. The Old Testament is my story whether I claim it or not. The Old Testament is also the story of our world today, as is illustrated daily at sporting events, in board rooms, elections, international relations, and on our streets where we all try to win at all costs.

The Christian Bible, however, moves to a new covenant, an invitation to abandon nation-building, past win-lose situations, and on to something greater than the individual. It invites *me* into *us*. The New Testament is about community and what we can accomplish together. It invites us to look to the good of the group – the family, the community, and the world, and to trust that as the group prospers, so will each member. It encourages us to join a larger body which the apostle Paul calls the Body of Christ. We are all gifted in different ways to serve as various parts of the body, and when we all do our part, the entire body prospers. We need to be careful, however, how we limit our definition of the collective body, or we fall back into our Old Testament ways. For the promise of the New Testament to manifest, the body must be all-inclusive or it will be incomplete and vulnerable. As soon

> ## *The New Testament invites* me *into* us.

as we begin excluding other groups, we tear away parts of the body. It does not matter if they are LGBTQ, Muslim, communist, or left-handed; inclusion is necessary. Some behavioral accommodation is required on all sides, but not excommunication. Whenever we wonder if someone is worthy of inclusion, we can ask, "Who would Jesus exclude?" The answer, of course, is that Jesus would not exclude anyone.

In the second half of my life, I find I am not so much interested in the nation of Greg as I am in the Body of Christ. The nation of Greg will fall, as do all nations, and another nation will consume it for its own narcissistic purposes. The nation of Greg must surrender and devote its resources to building the Body, as described in the New Testament. We can and must do better. One place to begin is to accept the Bible as our story.

2. The Kingdom of Heaven is Near

Now after John was arrested, Jesus came to Galilee, proclaiming the good news of God, and saying, "The time is fulfilled, and the kingdom of God has come near; repent, and believe the good news."
Mark 1:14-15

I do not know how I missed it, but somewhere in my childhood, and reinforced throughout my life, was the concept that heaven and hell were faraway places where we would go after we die. Heaven was somewhere above, and hell was somewhere below. Heaven was a paradise where we would be reunited with long-lost relatives, and hell was a place of eternal punishment where we would go if we did not live a life on earth worthy of heaven.

I believe the church I grew up in perpetuated these images and many churches today do the same. In spite of insisting we are saved by grace, as the apostle Paul proclaimed, there is still an element of needing to *earn* our salvation present in too many religious discussions. The threat of hell is ever near for those who do not give enough money to the right causes, live an acceptable lifestyle, vote for certain candidates, or regularly attend the right kind of church. Thankfully, many churches recognize the inclusivity God. If God is the God of any of us, God is the God of all and will not be limited by our imperfect, individual perceptions.

The first recorded words of Jesus in the Gospels of Matthew and Mark, and repeated throughout the Gospels, are that the kingdom of God – heaven – is near. We consistently overlook that teaching. For all the speculation about possible states of being after we die, we completely ignore that heaven and hell are present realities in our world right now, today, this moment, and in this place! Speculation about the future comes at the expense of the blessings of the now. Eternity stretches out in all directions from wherever we are at any point in time, and from that point we can experience heaven, or we can experience hell. The choice is ours because we are co-creators with God of the world we experience.

> *If God is the God of any of us, God is the God of all of us.*

Finding heaven on earth is challenging because there are so many attractive distractions that entice us to look in other directions, like possessions, positions, and power. The earth is a beautiful place with many lovely experiences, but few of them are eternal. Finding hell on earth, however, is much easier. There are many opportunities to be consumed by illness, financial straits, disabilities, loneliness, and broken hearts. When we focus on our suffering – and everyone suffers – we lose another moment in which we could experience heaven. Jesus invites us to repent (turn around) and enter into the Good News – right here, right now.

3. Hope Springs Eternal

Always be ready to make your defense to anyone who demands from you an accounting for the hope that is in you; yet do it with gentleness and reverence. 1 Peter 3:15b-16a

There is a huge difference between hope and wishful thinking. Hope is grounded in knowledge and experience, not uninformed optimism. At Christmas we may *wish* for a new video gaming system, nice jewelry, or a family board game, but we *hope* for love in our families, rebirth in ourselves, and peace on earth. This is the essential difference between hope and a wish. Most of what we wish for is temporal, where our hopes look to the long-term.

The leaders we most willingly choose to follow are full of hope. No one is inspired by a pessimist – cynically amused, maybe, but not inspired. Most pessimists prefer to be called *realists*, meaning their view of life is based on what they consider reality. Unfortunately for themselves and others, their view of reality tends to be a small, fatalistic one. Pessimists and realists believe that for every good thing that happens to us, something bad must occur in order to balance things out. When life is good we need to be cautious because there will be hell to pay later. Theirs is a philosophy of limitation, not a recognition of the abundance from which we were created.

Certainly, we need to be aware that with life comes death, with joy comes sorrow, and with light comes dark. They are parts of the same reality. It is not that we must pay for our joy with sorrow, but in order to fully experience joy we must also embrace the sorrow that is sometimes a part of it. It is when we refuse to fully experience life that it hurts, that it leaves us sad, or that we feel we cannot go on. Joy does not bring sorrow any more than day brings night. They are manifestations of the same reality. They go together. One cannot exist without the other, so trying to separate them or experience one without the other is impossible. Hope does not tell us to be wary of life because death always follows. Hope assures us that with life comes death and *both* are good when experienced to the fullest.

Looking to the future with a confident hope frees us to live fully in the present. We *know* the future will bring its blessings, challenges, and solutions, so we need not allow tomorrow's possible calamities or yesterday's injustices to prevent us from fully experiencing today. From God's perspective, the future is now, and it is good. Because we exist in time and space, we co-create the details and experience them as they unfold.

> *It is when we refuse to fully experience life that it hurts.*

When the day comes that our physical body gives out, we *hope* for a new life that retains everything good from our days on earth and places it in a new life beyond. For those who know the Gospel, this is not wishful thinking; rather, it is the hope that is in us, rooted in our knowledge of and experience with God. Like a spring fed by an unseen source of pure water, life springs eternal; and life is good. *That* is the source of our hope.

There is *always* reason for hope, because hope springs eternal.

4. *Faith Heals*

Then suddenly a woman who had been suffering from hemorrhages for twelve years came up behind him and touched the fringe of his cloak, for she said to herself, "If I only touch his cloak, I will be made well." Jesus turned, and seeing her he said, "Take heart, daughter; your faith has made you well." And instantly the woman was made well. Matthew 9:20-22

The relationship between healing and faith is difficult to understand, impossible to predict, and a connection Jesus mentions many times throughout his ministry. He often healed someone, only to give credit to that person's faith. I used to believe Jesus was being modest. After all, he seems like a humble man. He credits faith with healing so many times, however, that I find myself rethinking his modesty. Dare we believe that faith truly does heal?

I have tried to apply faith with instances of serious illness in people I know, but with ambiguous results. I remember praying hard for my mother's recovery from a stroke. She had been a healthy, determined woman, and I could easily visualize her fighting her way back to health. But she never did. Rather, her health steadily declined, and she passed away 10 weeks later. The times when an unlikely healing has occurred, and there have been a few, I find myself wondering if it was a God-healing or a talented physician. Clearly, God works through the hands and hearts of God's people. If I were keeping score, however, of the number of times I believe my faith brought the outcome I prayed for, faith would be losing by a landslide. Is this due to my weak faith, or my lack of understanding about healing?

Not all healings are equal, nor are they all physical. When we pray for healing, we are generally praying for restoration to a prior state of being. We pray for what we, in our limited understanding, believe to be the best outcome. Do we possess the perspective to know what is best in any situation? There are numerous examples of physical healings in the Bible, but we can assume all those people died of something, eventually. There are also instances where God does not heal the physical ailment of a faithful person – Paul comes to mind. Paul used his infirmity as a reminder of his total reliance upon grace. Even Jesus, the night before his crucifixion, prays for God to "take this cup from me." Ultimately, he yields by saying, "Not my will, but yours be done." I have often wondered why God did not rescue Jesus from the cross. But wait, Jesus was rescued via his resurrection. He was not, however, rescued in the way we humans would have requested.

> *Not all healings are equal, nor are they all physical.*

If faith truly does heal, there is a lot of pressure on us to be well. Wellness becomes a faith issue that is under our control, instead of our being victimized by illnesses we can do nothing about. Most of us find a comfortable balance between faith healing and utilizing more contemporary forms of health care, depending on the malady. Either way, faith is our connection to God. It is the thread by which our humanity connects to the divine. Faith assures us there is more to life than what we see, hear, touch, taste, and smell – there is more beyond our human knowledge and efforts. Would God grant us a desire contrary to our ultimate good? As a parent, there were many times I refused to grant a desire of my children, knowing they were better off without having their wish granted.

What is out there, and how and when it may or may not bless us remains a mystery. Dare we believe that faith heals? Dare we believe it does not?

5. Alone Time is Important

And whenever you pray, do not be like the hypocrites; for they love to stand and pray in the synagogues and at the street corners, so that they may be seen by others. Truly I tell you, they have received their reward. But whenever you pray, go into your room and shut the door and pray to your Father who is in secret; and your Father who sees in secret will reward you. Matthew 6:5-6

Growing up, I learned to pray with others. My father prayed before family meals, and our pastor led us in prayer at church. The Lord's Prayer, spoken collectively, was a common fixture in worship. There was also a bedtime prayer, spoken in unison with a parent:

Now I lay me down to sleep, I pray the Lord my soul to keep;
If I should die before I wake, I pray the Lord my soul to take.

I remember sitting in church as a child wondering how the preacher could possibly think of so much to pray about. The prayers seemed to drone on, and it was very difficult to remain focused. I kept my eyes clamped shut as long as I could, afraid someone might catch peeking. Prayer was not very comforting in those days.

I am not certain when I learned to pray by myself, but however it happened, time alone with God quickly became my favorite method of prayer. I am an introvert, so time alone is a necessary part of my life, anyway. Jesus modeled alone time with God for us. Many times in the Gospels, he goes off alone to pray. Like spending time with a close, intimate friend, words are not always necessary in prayer. In fact, I find more of my prayers as I age to be of the silent type. I have no idea what I could verbalize to God that God does not already know better than I can put into words. There are times, however, when a spoken prayer can help us organize whatever is on our mind. Even so, being in God's presence is enough. In his letter to the Romans, Paul writes, "The Spirit helps us in our weakness, for we do not know how to pray as we ought." I find

> *Preach the Gospel always.*
> *When necessary, use words.*
> St. Francis of Assisi

this to be true. In his first letter to the church at Thessalonica, Paul writes, "Pray without ceasing." This seems to be an encouragement toward wordless prayer – staying in communion with God at all times, but not necessarily with words. St. Francis of Assisi[2] reportedly said, "Preach the Gospel always. When necessary, use words." This applies to prayer, too. We can remain in constant contact with God without an on-going verbal dialogue. In fact, our dialogue makes it impossible to hear what God might be trying to tell us.

My point is not that we should always pray silently; rather it is that *alone-time* with God is important. We need worry less about *what* we say and more about being present. Whether in meditation, contemplation, reflection, yoga, or any number of other methods, a quiet mind attunes our awareness to God's presence. If Jesus needed quiet, alone time with God in order to center himself, recharge, and reconnect in the days prior to television and the internet, think how much more we need it today.

6. *Words are Metaphors*

Welcome with meekness the implanted word that has the power to save your souls. But be doers of the word, and not merely hearers who deceive themselves. James 1:21b-22

There are many words that, when spoken to another, create a visual sense of shared meaning, at least in general terms. For example, if I say, "I see a large rock," you would envision something hard, inanimate, and bigger than a closed fist. The word *rock* is a metaphor for the broad swath of reality that we call rocks, but the word is *not* the reality. There is another category of words that point to something less tangible. For example, if I say, "I *love* her," or "That is a *beautiful* tree," you might be able to imagine the emotion I express but there will be little or no shared visualization of the detail behind the word. The important point here is that words are metaphors, or our *names* for different things we encounter in our environment. Words are *not* the things themselves. Much of the information in the Bible falls into the latter category of words – those that point us in a direction, but cannot give us the individualistic experience they describe. We see this manifesting in our relationships, where I use certain words to express something and my partner hears those same words, but envisions something very different.

While many believe the Bible is the *inspired* word of God, as 2 Timothy 3:16 tells us, God did not *dictate* the Bible to its writers. I believe the writers had a wordless God-encounter that they graciously put into words for our sake. The words recorded were their own, however, not God's. Verbally, our God is mostly silent; yet God inspires us with regularity. Trying to contain that

> *Metaphors may express truth more accurately than facts.*

inspiration in words to share with others is difficult at best. Trying to describe that inspiration in a way that allows others to attain the identical experience is essentially impossible.

So, if words are only metaphors, dare we believe anything in the Bible? Certainly so! Metaphors are full of meaning and truth, providing important context for facts, which too often leave us feeling cold and confused. Being a metaphor does not mean something is not true – in fact, metaphors may express truth more accurately and on several different levels. Attempting to understand something deep and powerful from a verbal description, as opposed to an actual experience, often leads to a shallow and partial understanding. We may understand the *letter* of the communication but completely miss its *meaning*. We must work to understand a metaphor. It invites us to wrestle with it, pondering what it says about God, about life, and about us. Seldom will answers come quickly or easily, and our understandings may change at different stages of our lives.

The beauty and purpose of metaphor is that it leads us on a journey of discovery, as opposed to a one-time destination. The goal of spiritual development is not to attain an intellectual understanding of the words, but to *experience* the Living Word to which the words point. Metaphors are much better suited to this latter task. The Living Word is implanted within every being, as the writer of James tells us. We need not strive to understand that Word as much as to allow it expression within and around us.

7. The Way Out is Through

Then Jesus said, "Father, forgive them; for they do not know what they are doing." Luke 23:34a
"I shouted out, who killed the Kennedys? When after all, it was you and me." Sympathy for the Devil, Mick Jagger and Keith Richards

We live in a violent time. Pundits of every persuasion speak with certainty about the causes and cures for the current violence. I am unconvinced. What I am listening for and not hearing is someone recognizing and accepting personal responsibility for a solution to the violence.

Long ago, I was taught that one cannot solve a problem without accepting some level of responsibility for its creation. Once I recognize my part in a problem, I am able to begin making meaningful changes that may actually have a positive impact. The change, however, must begin within me. If not, I join the legions of complainers, finger-pointers, hand-wringers, pontificators, and other reactionaries that only perpetuate the problem, often with the best of intentions. As

Christians, we have the audacity to claim Jesus took the sins of the world – past, present, and future – to the cross to purchase our salvation. Do we understand the nature of that sacrifice, however? Do we know how to apply it in practical ways? One lesson of the cross is how to participate in the reconciling of social ills. What Jesus modeled for us is this: *The way out is through.*

Jesus, an entirely innocent victim, knew a horrible death he did not deserve was waiting. He would endure the worst torture that humanity knew how to inflict at the time. The social systems of Jesus' day, like today, were unjust and violent. They wrongly believed, as we believe, that progress – however the culture defines it – comes by force. Jesus recognized the corrupt underlying system and, in his humanity, refused to participate in or perpetuate it. Once accused, he did not get defensive or try to shift the condemnation onto others. He knew the only way out of the situation – to begin a social healing process – was to accept his condemnation, take up his cross, and go *through* it. In that act of civil disobedience, Jesus modeled what happens when we go through a difficult challenge – we come out the other side changed. All efforts to avoid, go around, or deny a problem leave it for another day.

What are my roles in today's issues? Where are my actions toward others discriminatory and unjust? Which of my cultural assumptions are repressive? How do my words exclude others from kinship as fellow children of God? Specifically, what am I doing, or *not doing*, that contributes to the problem? As a Christian, American (the only category of American without an ethnically-based prefix), heterosexual, white male, I have no significant experience with discrimination. I am near the top of the socio-economic ladder by accident of birth. Until I understand and accept my role in perpetuating a violent, discriminatory culture, I remain firmly a part of the problem – without ever raising a fist or pulling a trigger.

From the cross, Jesus looked with mercy on those who inflicted the horrible injustice upon him and asked that God forgive them. They did not know what they were doing; and neither do we. The spiral of violence we find ourselves in will only be solved when a critical mass of people accept responsibility for their part, say

> *One cannot solve a problem without accepting some level of responsibility for its creation.*

"Enough," take up their cross, and go *through* the problem, including acceptance of its inevitable consequences.

Martin Luther King, Jr.[1], said, "Darkness cannot drive out darkness; only love can do that." In these dark times, only love can carry us through to the other side. We underestimate how rare that sort of love is, however, let alone the level of sacrifice and focus it requires. Not all of us will survive the challenge, at least not physically, but deeply-imbedded social ills require much sacrifice for the future good. Jesus showed us the way. Non-violent leaders like Dr. King and Mahatma Gandhi gave their lives for it. They faced evil head on, absorbed the worst evil could throw at them, and came out triumphant on the other side.

8. The Road to Nowhere is the Road to Everywhere

I will lead the blind by a road they do not know, by paths they have not known I will guide them. I will turn darkness before them into light, the rough places into level ground. Isaiah 42:16

Several decades ago, a friend and mentor introduced me to Eastern philosophy. Much of it seemed nonsensical at first. It was full of circular, impossible-to-fathom sayings that were intriguing, but seemed not to lead anywhere, at least not that I could see. Being a child of the West, I learned to discern fact from fiction, right from wrong, north from south. There were important distinctions to recognize and lines to be drawn between this and that. The great Eastern teachers' lessons were mostly vague and noncommittal. What drew me to their words, however, was the way they grabbed something inside of me and held on until I engaged, like a wrestling match with one's shadow. A paraphrase of one of my favorite sayings (from an unremembered author) is: "If you cannot find happiness where you are standing, where do you expect to wander in search of it?" In retrospect, that sounds exactly like the sort of thing Jesus would say. Of course, Jesus *was* from the Middle East.

Many of us feel we simply must change our physical location, our job, or our significant other in order to find happiness or personal fulfillment. Sometimes, as in cases of professional opportunities or abusive relationships, that may be true. If we have always dreamed of living near an ocean or in the mountains, staying in Kansas may not be a good choice. The point, however, is that happiness, fulfillment, and contentment are primarily internal states that have little to do with our external environment. Often, when we feel we simply must go somewhere else, we are only running from something inside ourselves that will follow us and manifest again, no matter how far away we run. At some point, we are better off to stay put, honestly and openly reflect on our life, and take the road to nowhere.

The road within is not an actual road; but it is a journey – a journey of self-discovery. Eastern philosophy helped me understand the importance of looking within for the source of love, strife, strength, and life in ways that my Western upbringing seemed to disavow. Virtual roads to happiness extend in every direction from where we stand at any given moment. These roads are internal, and we find them as we face our own demons and learn

> *Happiness, fulfillment, and contentment are primarily internal states that have little to do with our external environment.*

to be content with what we have, even as we strive for more. Happiness and contentment are not *out there*, somewhere; they are always *in here*. Our creator planted them where they lurk closer than our next breath. It may seem like bad news that we cannot run from ourselves. The good news is that we take the road to happiness with us wherever we go, even on the road to nowhere.

9. Brokenness Leads to Wholeness

The sacrifice acceptable to God is a broken spirit; a broken and contrite heart, O God, you will not despise. Psalm 51:17

The eggshell must be broken at the right time for the chick to emerge. The caterpillar must be broken and bound for the butterfly to emerge. The skin of reptiles must split open for them to grow into their next stage of life. And, painful as it often is, our current state of life must be broken in order for us to move to the next stage of our development. Life is a series of deaths and rebirths, and being broken is at the heart of the process. I do not enjoy it; but I can either be broken willingly, or I can fight it tooth and nail, but broken I will be.

The central problem is that a full and satisfied heart lacks the motivation to change. When we are satisfied, we fight to maintain the status quo. We do whatever we can to minimize change, even when a change is necessary to improve the lot of our self and others. In political contests, one candidate is often portrayed as the "change" agent and the other as the "establishment." The former makes the case that the current system is broken and needs to be rebuilt. The latter claims the system is good enough to provide a solid foundation from which to improve and only requires strategic tweaking. In many cases, who we favor depends on the level of brokenness of our current state in life. While I do not advocate change for the sake of change, brokenness, in its time, is necessary for the sake of growth.

I am not advocating that we break a perfectly good life – destruction is a process that happens naturally enough, with or without our prodding. When we feel the status quo of our life starting to bend, however, it may be time to embrace a change. The bending may be the Spirit moving in our lives in a way that will lead us to a new level of wholeness. Sometimes, that may mean breaking away from negative influences by ending a toxic relationship, leaving a disrespectful employer, or receiving help for an addiction. Other times, we need to break away from our own inertia by intentionally committing ourselves to

> *A full and satisfied heart lacks the motivation to change.*

a new relationship, forming new, healthier habits, or beginning a regular prayer or meditation practice.

Sometimes we have already been broken, but we have not yet embraced the new possibilities. We, like Humpty Dumpty, have fallen off the wall, and we expend energy and resources trying to rebuild what once *was* instead of taking stock of what is *now*. Being broken opens a new world of possibilities for us, but we will never see the possible until we willingly let go of the shattered past. An old saying goes, "If it ain't broke, don't fix it." There are times, however, when we do need to break something in order to move ahead in life. At the very least, when we feel unavoidable change coming, we can perhaps find peace knowing whatever the shape of the post-change life, there will always be new opportunities and blessings.

10. Sin is Separation

My little children, I am writing these things to you so that you may not sin. But if anyone does sin, we have an advocate with the Father, Jesus Christ the righteous; and he is the atoning sacrifice for our sins, and not for ours only but also for the sins of the whole world. 1 John 2:1-2

At an early age, I learned I was a sinner. I believed my thoughts and actions were unacceptable to God, and the only thing I could do about it was try to hide my awful nature. I pretended to be a "good, little boy" to friends and relatives, and especially to people at church, so they would consider me one of them – the *good* and the *chosen* – instead of the wretched misfit I thought myself to be. I am not certain how I came to believe I was such a terrible anomaly – I suspect it was at church. I do not recall my parents instilling an aberrant self-belief, but sin was a weekly topic in the church where I grew up. That God knew my every thought and watched my every action convinced me I would undoubtedly spend eternity in hell. As an adult, I cautiously came to believe I was no worse than other folks I knew, so if I were condemned to hell, I would be in good company. I realized that everyone sins, and sin is a common and shared characteristic, rather than something that was a struggle only for me.

Today, however, I view sin differently. Viewing sin as *separation* opened an entirely new understanding of sin for me: Sin is what sets us apart – apart from God and apart from each other. When I sin against you, I do something that divides us, something that harms our relationship. In order to restore our relationship, I must confess my sin (admit I did wrong), repent (meaning *turn around* or change or apologize), and seek your forgiveness (ask you to reengage our relationship). That sounds like a pretty natural and common progression in any relationship worth maintaining.

Traditionally, we track the *original sin* to the Garden of Eden, with Adam and Eve defying God's command not to eat the fruit of the Tree of the Knowledge of Good and Evil. Their punishment was expulsion from the Garden, where they had enjoyed a direct, unfettered relationship with God. In other words, they *separated* from God. I now believe the original sin was not the eating of the fruit, but the leaving of the Garden itself – their *willful separation* from God. The very act of a soul taking on flesh and blood and becoming human is an act of separation – a

> *The illusion of separation is the true original sin.*

sinful act, if you will – because as humans we enter a reality that appears individualistic and separate. From our human vantage point, we cannot see God, nor can we see our interconnectedness with each other. We believe ourselves to be separate, independent entities, and that separation is the illusion at the root of most of our problems. In my opinion, the illusion of separation is the true original sin.

At times, we Christians are quick to point out the sins of others and equally remiss in pointing out the divine grace and forgiveness that is as close as their next breath. In the very act of judging another, we commit sin by driving a wedge between another and ourselves. Sin, because it creates division with others, is its own punishment. God need not punish us further. In fact, God reaches out to rejoin with us. When I was a child, I had a miserable self-image because I did not feel worthy to be in close relationship with others. Yet, close relationship is what we were created for and is the reality behind the illusion. Without it, we are miserable.

11. Sin is its own Punishment

Do not sin anymore, so that nothing worse happens to you.
John 5:14c

In my opinion, there are a number of misconceptions about sin. One common misconception is that sin is offensive to God. We are created in the image of God, and it is an inescapable consequence of our physical being that we sin. God may not be amused, but God is not surprised. A second misconception is that God keeps track of our sins and, like a big Santa-in-the-Sky, one sin too many puts us on the dreaded Bad Child List. Another misconception is that we must somehow be purified of our sinful nature in order to be loved and accepted by God.

For me, one way to view sin is like hitting my thumb with a hammer. There is no one to blame except me, and the resulting pain serves as an effective teacher to become more attentive in the future. As I have written elsewhere, sin is that which separates us from God and others. God does not abandon us in our sin, but *we separate ourselves* from our participation in God's loving presence as a natural consequence of our sin. If we believe, as I do, that God lives in, through, and with us, then God must suffer *with* us in our sin. If we become obese and live with diabetes or other health issues, God suffers with us. If we commit a crime that lands us in jail, God joins us in our cell. Similarly, when we suffer an illness or condition with no traceable connection to anything we have ever done, God never abandons us. So, the consequences of sin are never just borne by us because God shares our burdens with us. God never *leaves* us, however, nor does God love us any less passionately. It is only our awareness of God's love that waxes and wanes.

Frequently, it is our suffering that motivates us to make needed changes. The Gospel is an invitation to grow toward Christ, to become evermore Christ-like. Paradoxically, our sin – at least the pain of separation it causes – motivates us to grow in ways that help us better

> *God does not abandon us in our sin, but we separate ourselves from our participation in God's loving presence as a natural consequence of our sin.*

experience God's presence. God neither wants nor wills our sin or suffering. But whenever we hurt, God crawls into the hole – or onto the cross – with us. Contrary to how it may feel at the time, God never runs *from* our suffering, God runs *to* it. And in our times of darkness, we find ourselves *craving* an ever nearer experience of the divine. We are motivated to transform those actions that separate us from what is good – our sin – and grow toward a life more expressive of loving union with God and others. Because sin is its own punishment, God neither has to keep track of our sin, nor specifically punish us for it. The price of sin is automatically included in the personal cost.

12. Meekness is not Weakness

Blessed are the meek, for they will inherit the earth.
Matthew 5:5

Among the definitions for the word *meek* are docile, spiritless, obsolete, and overly submissive or compliant. These do not sound particularly holy, given that Jesus says the meek will inherit the earth. The word *meek,* however, can also mean humble, gentle, and kind. As we wonder why Jesus held meekness in such high esteem, the latter definitions may lead us to a better answer. Certainly, Jesus modeled these positive characteristics of meekness.

To say that the meek will inherit the earth seems like a paradox of giant proportions. As we look around our world today, we see a small percentage of people controlling the largest share of the earth's bounty. My perception of the very rich is hardly meek. I see people who are bold, aggressive, assertive, opportunistic, and hard-driving risk-takers. While some may be humble, gentle, and kind in their private lives, their stereotyped public persona is very different.

Meekness, in any of its forms, is not encouraged in personal development by our current culture. We have popular, anti-meekness bits of folk wisdom like, "Go for the gusto," or "You only live once," or "Just do it!" I suspect the type of meekness Jesus advocated for was not the sniveling, whiney, frightened, spiritless, spineless sort we often associate with the word today. Rather, the meek who will inherit the earth are the strong but humble, gentle, and kind people who place others' needs above their own. These are common traits found in women and men who model their lives after Jesus.

One difficulty in understanding this concept is our understanding of what it means to *inherit* the earth. If our desired inheritance is one of vast riches, nice homes, fancy cars, lavish clothing, or a private jet, then meekness is not likely to get us there. These riches are transient, in that they do not last beyond our time on earth. There are other riches uniquely of the earth, however, that imprint

> *The meek who will inherit the earth are the strong, but humble, gentle, and kind people who place others' needs above their own.*

on our souls and, I believe, shape our existence beyond this life. For example, experiencing long-term, deeply-loving relationships, making a positive difference in someone else's life, and working for causes greater than our own. These are opportunities this life gives that are available to all, but are only sought and valued by those with a propensity towards meekness. Only the meek will inherit the blessings of these more lasting gifts of the earth – everyone else will forego them for something more material.

13. Judgment is Self-Incriminating

Do not judge, so that you may not be judged. For with the judgment you make you will be judged, and the measure you give will be the measure you get. Why do you see the speck in your neighbor's eye, but do not notice the log in your own eye? Or how can you say to your neighbor, "Let me take the speck out of your eye,' while the log is in your own eye? You hypocrite, first take the log out of your own eye, and then you will see clearly to take the speck out of your neighbor's eye. Matthew 7:1-5

I remember being taught that whenever I point a finger at someone, three fingers point back at me. It was a lesson in judgment – as in, be careful when tempted to criticize others. Most of us are at least partially blind to our own shortcomings. Author William Wharton[3] writes: "What we all tend to complain about most in other people are those things we don't like about ourselves."

I am ashamed to confess how judgmental I can be. I not only judge the words and actions of others, I judge their motives. There is no way for me to know the motivations of another. As individuals and as a society, we gossip ruthlessly, we bully, and we discriminate. Rendering harsh judgments has become such a common and accepted practice we hardly realize we are doing it. When we judge behind another's back, we do it not so much to tear others down as to build ourselves up. How did we become so insecure as to build our own self-esteem at the expense of others?

The tendency to judge others is not new. Two thousand years ago, Jesus spoke harshly about casting judgment, telling us to attend to the "log" in our own eye before worrying about the "speck" in the eye of another. We will be judged by the same measure we use to judge others. He called us "hypocrites." None of us are perfect or righteous enough to stand in judgment of another, especially when that criticism is unfair and unfounded.

This is why I grow so weary of political campaigns – candidates consistently try to build themselves up by pronouncing judgments of unworthiness upon their opponents. The fact that I am so bothered by this, unfortunately, is probably an indication that I tend to do the same thing. Ugh. Perhaps it is like a balloon (filled with hot air) and being squeezed at one end, causing the other end to expand. Whenever I deny or repress undesirable parts of myself, those thoughts or actions enter my awareness through others.

> *None of us are perfect or righteous enough to stand in judgement of another.*

One of the clearest commands of Jesus was to love each other. Mother Teresa of Calcutta[4] said, "If you judge people, you have no time to love them." This may capture the core evil of judgment – that we cannot love and judge at the same time. Perhaps, instead of criticizing another, we should be looking within for something we can improve in ourselves. In the words of Fr. Richard Rohr[5], "The best criticism of the bad is the practice of the better."

14. Our Possessions Possess Us

Do not store up for yourselves treasures on earth, where moth and rust consume and where thieves break in and steal; but store up for yourselves treasures in heaven, where neither moth nor rust consumes and where thieves do not break in and steal. For where your treasure is, there your heart will be also. Matthew 6:19-21

My wife and I are blessed to live in a large house on five acres of land. It is located in the rolling hills south of Lawrence, Kansas, among a beautiful mix of field and forest. We enjoy stunning sunsets on a regular basis and can view much of the night sky that is invisible to our city brethren. Even when our children were home, we had plenty of room for everyone and everyone's *stuff.* Musical instruments, clothes, books, music, furniture – you name it, we probably have it.

As I age, I notice that much of what I was excited to possess in earlier days requires an amount of time and resources that is disproportionate to its current value to me. So many things I simply had to have in my younger years now have me wondering what I was thinking. Even trying to thin out the excess, however, is a difficult process. First, one never knows when something might come in handy, or when a friend or family member might need it. Second, there is sentimental value in much of what we have. It is difficult to throw things like old photographs away no matter how old and faded they have become, and no matter that we cannot remember the names of many of the people in the pictures. Third, passing things on to others means cleaning, moving, and organizing. It is often easier to hoard (or to leave the problem for my children).

Jesus warned us not to store up for ourselves treasures of the earth. Actually, I think his point has to do with what we *value*, more than what we possess. If we keep things we do not need, however, we are assigning a value to them. There are reasons that holding onto stuff in excess of our need is inconsistent with Christian teaching. First, there are those who really *need* some of what gathers dust in our homes. Second, there are maintenance costs associated with everything we keep, and those costs are resources unavailable for other, more important uses. Third, and most important in my opinion, *our possessions possess us*.

> *There are maintenance costs associated with everything we keep.*

In too many ways, I am a slave to my possessions. When I spend my weekends maintaining my large yard or trying to keep the contents of our big house in order, I have neither time nor energy to dedicate to other needs of my family, friends, and community. If I must first rearrange my old stuff to make room for new stuff, I accomplish nothing of value – for myself or others. If my heart – my time, my attention, and my God-given resources – is consumed in caring for my *stuff*, where, when, and how can I have a heart for others? It is a challenging spiritual dilemma, and one I will likely wrestle with for the rest of my life.

15. Non-Violence is Non-Negotiable

"You have heard that it was said, 'An eye for an eye and a tooth for a tooth.' But I say to you, Do not resist an evildoer. But if anyone strikes you on the right cheek, turn the other also."
Matthew 5:38-39

I do not know how I missed it, but Jesus modeled unwavering non-violence. That would not be an issue for me, except that Jesus' most frequently repeated directive was "Follow me." Based on Christian teachings, as recorded in the Gospels, if we are to be followers of Christ, non-violence is non-negotiable. I cannot imagine any way that we can justify violence of any sort as being consistent with Jesus' teaching.

We were born into violent times, however, so what are we to do, turn the other cheek? Apparently so (see Matthew 5:39). What about wars? What about those in our military, charged to protect our national interests in sometimes-violent ways? Let me assert that I do not condemn those serving in our military, past or present. These faithful and brave servants do what is necessary for the rest of us to live as we do, and God bless them for it. Even so, how do we reconcile any sort of violence with the Christian teaching of non-violence? I think the key lies within us, as individuals, in our personal lives. Soldiers do not create the conditions that lead to violence; leaders do that. And we elect and support those leaders. Ultimately, the responsibility is yours and mine, and in more ways than one.

Violence is a daily occurrence on our streets, in our workplaces, and in our homes. I am told that a shared characteristic of essentially every violent person is a violent upbringing. Typically, a violent or absent father, who himself likely experienced a violent childhood, demonstrated that violence is how one gets what one wants. If things are not going as one wishes, a few loud, nasty words, a punch, or a weapon may help bring the desired outcome. Road rage, bullying, name-calling, and gossip are all current examples of indirect violence. We justify them as not *really* hurting anyone, but is that true? At the very least, our harsh reactions – even when they are not physical – contribute to the violent environment of our world.

> *A shared characteristic of essentially every violent person is a violent upbringing.*

Violence begins at home. If we are to manifest a non-violent world, it must begin within. Widespread non-violence will not happen in my lifetime, and probably not in my children's lifetimes, either. But it can and must begin with me – and you. When I feel my anger or frustration beginning to build, I need to examine my choices prior to reacting. What is the most appropriate response that does not lead to or perpetuate violence? How can I act to help end what is likely the latest in a long string of violent acts, possibly dating back many generations? In what ways can I commit to physical, emotional, and intellectual non-violence in my own part of the world? Within my heart is where non-violence must first manifest.

16. There is a Third Way

When they kept on questioning him, he straightened up and said to them, "Let anyone among you who is without sin be the first to throw a stone at her." John 8:7

I imagine the excitement building in Jerusalem. The crowds were ready for some gruesome entertainment. A woman had been caught in the act of adultery, and the Law was clear – she should be stoned to death. Stoning was a religious mandate that the crowds could participate in. The pious, religious authorities were there, and the people were ready to begin, stones in hand. There was one problem, however – Jesus. The Pharisees, hoping to trap Jesus into denying the legitimacy of the Law of Moses, asked him whether the woman should be stoned. Jesus bent over and wrote something on the ground. When they continued pressing him, he suggested that the one among them without sin throw the first stone. One by one, the people dropped their stones and walked away.

Jesus modeled a *third way*, or a higher truth. The Law was clear, and the Hebrew people believed their salvation was dependent on obedience to that Law. Jesus did not challenge the Law. Instead, he transformed the situation by challenging the justice of one sinner punishing another. It was a brilliant move. It was a third way that did not deny the Law, nor did it condone the woman's behavior. It forced everyone present to examine his or her own lives and actions. There may not have been other adulterers in the crowd, but there were no sinless purists, either.

We have a tendency to reduce our choices to two options – right or wrong, light or dark, male or female, condone or condemn. There is a significant portion of each day that is neither light nor dark, however, but somewhere in between. The same is true for our lives. There

> *When we narrow our choices to two, we limit the possibilities.*

are circumstances where no obvious options are clearly right or wrong, depending on the perspective from which they are experienced. When we narrow our choices to two, supporting one and denying the other, we limit the possibilities of our existence and perpetuate an either-or world. Thus, the importance of the third way.

Finding the Third Way is seldom quick or easy, but is always inclusive and respectful of peoples and traditions. The third way may not be any one particular group's preferred way forward, but it will allow all people to progress. The third way may not achieve perfection, but it will move us closer to a just and righteous society. One of the many shortcomings of our two-solution focus is that we become more vested in defending our position than in solving our problems. When the only tool we have in our possession is a rock, our options are limited by the tool at hand.

17. Marginalized Lives Matter

"Come, you that are blessed by my Father, inherit the kingdom prepared for you from the foundation of the world; for I was hungry and you gave me food, I was thirsty and you gave me something to drink, I was a stranger and you welcomed me, I was naked and you gave me clothing, I was sick and you took care of me, I was in prison and you visited me. Truly I tell you, just as you did it to one of the least of these who are members of my family, you did it to me." Matthew 25:34b-36,40b

A marginalized person is one who is at the edges of society – not outside *per se*, but not exerting influence or experiencing the blessing of full inclusion, either. Marginalized people need advocates, or people firmly within the societal circle to work on their behalf. If they have no such representation, they often end up forgotten, shunned, and disenfranchised.

Before proceeding further, let me confess that I a member of the privileged class who perpetuates the current cultural norms – fully abled, white, heterosexual, American, and male. I write this as a way to better understand how to be a part of the solution. In 2016, the *Black Lives Matter* movement formed in reaction to the marginalization of people of color. Though given equal rights under the law in the 1960's, the arrest and incarceration rates, unemployment and murder rates, discrimination and racial profiling, and the prevalence of poverty remain unacceptably high for the African-American race as a whole. Some tried to make the movement more inclusive by saying *All Lives Matter*, which is true, of course, but it misses the point. In his blog, Pierre Khawand[6] writes, "When everything is a priority, nothing is a priority." A society can only rise as high as it is willing to lift and include the least within it. In a truly just and fair world, there would be no need to focus more attention on certain segments. Unfortunately, that is not our world. All lives will matter when no lives are marginalized.

Marginalization is not limited to a specific race. The homeless, the poor, Americans whose first language is not English, the variously challenged, and the addicted, all are too often kept on the fringes of our society – hidden from view as if they were invisible and

> *A society can only rise as high as it is willing to lift and include the least within it.*

unimportant. Who will stand for the marginalized? Who will advocate with power for the LGBTQ community, or the girl with the unwanted pregnancy – or her unborn child? Who will stand in the gap with sleeves rolled up and work for a just and caring world? *Jesus makes clear that it should be us.* In the passage above from Matthew he lists the marginalized of his day and says, "Just as you did it to one of the least of these who are members of my family, you did it to me." Can it be any clearer? I do not know how I can overlook it. When I walk by a person in an unfortunate circumstance, when I witness an injustice, when I see someone broken-hearted or lonely, I see a broken member of Jesus' family. That person is loved and cherished by the one I claim to follow. If I pass them by in their hour of need, I pass Jesus by in his.

We marginalize others when we fear them, when we ignore them, or when we treat them differently than we desire to be treated. One solution that is deceptively simple, but monumentally challenging, is written in Matthew 7:12: "In everything, do to others as you would have them do to you." As we do to others, we do also to Jesus.

18. There is Power in Powerlessness

But he said to me, "My grace is sufficient for you, for power is made perfect in weakness." So, I will boast all the more gladly of my weaknesses, so that the power of Christ may dwell in me. Therefore I am content with weaknesses, insults, hardships, persecutions, and calamities for the sake of Christ; for whenever I am weak, then I am strong. 2 Corinthians 12:9-10

Our pain is exacerbated by feeling powerless over it. Physical or emotional hurt is one thing, but when there is nothing we can do to ease that pain, our level of misery increases significantly. When we work in a hostile environment, or when we live in abusive surroundings, we may not see very many good alternatives. Further, we may believe the status quo is preferable to the unknown. While this holding to what is known may seem a logical choice, unpleasant as it is, that is exactly the attitude that prevents us from stepping out of the old and into a new existence. Positive change requires us to give up whatever illusion of power we may believe we have over our current situation.

The condition of powerlessness is an illusion, however, or at best is only a partial truth. The fact that we cannot exercise control over a situation does not mean there is no power at work for our good. Scripture and experience assures us that *all things* work together for good. Powerless situations may actually prove to us that the power we thought we had was imaginary. In reality,

> *Experiencing powerlessness forces us to rethink our view and understanding of the world.*

we are not nearly as powerful over the flow of our days as we believe. Certainly, we have influence over the impact our environment has on us, but time marches relentlessly on in ways we can do little to change. I remember a Superman movie where something disastrous happened and Superman made the earth reverse its orbit long enough to turn back time so he could change the outcome. We have no such power; we can only change our outlook. Experiencing powerlessness, however, forces us to rethink our view and understanding of the world. It is only when something we have held to be true and good is shown to be false that we open our mind to other, higher possibilities. It is only when life has become unbearably unpleasant that we willingly let go of the old and open ourselves to something new. We are creatures of comfort and familiarity, and we go to great lengths to preserve both, often at our own peril.

Powerlessness is an illusion, though, because the power of God's Spirit flowing through us is always at work. Indeed, without that Spirit, life is not possible. It is our spiritual oxygen. We will not knowingly experience the power of the Spirit, however, until we let go of the illusion that we are in control. As long as we feel in control, we are not open to surrendering to a higher source of control. It is only in our powerlessness that we experience God's power.

19. Exclusion Leads to Implosion

And as he sat at dinner in Levi's house, many tax collectors and sinners were also sitting with Jesus and his disciples – for there were many who followed him. Mark 2:15

I am not fluent in astrophysics, so forgive my pseudo-scientific musings, but there seems to be agreement that our universe is expanding at an ever-increasing rate. There are elements within our universe, however, that are contracting. Black holes are former stars that have died and imploded into themselves, retaining all their mass, but in an infinitely small space. Anything near a black hole is sucked into that hole and cannot escape, not even light.

Some churches remind me of a black hole. They worship what seems to me a very small God, and they exclude large swaths of humanity from those they say are redeemed. They believe themselves to be God's "chosen ones," and everyone else will burn in Hell. They identify certain words that must be said, rituals that must be practiced, rules that must be followed, and they are certain in their knowledge that they are right and everyone else is wrong. These churches, not unlike a black hole, suck everything into themselves so that nothing good can escape, not even love or light. I believe this type of exclusion would cause Jesus to roll over in his tomb (if he were still there).

Jesus was inclusive and rejected no one. In fact, much of the criticism he received had to do with the choices he made in followers. He hung out with sinners and those usually excluded from recognized social circles – prostitutes, tax collectors, fishermen, adulterers, lepers, and foreigners. In fact, the only group he consistently criticized was the religious elite – those who sought to exclude others from their pious circles. This was the group that made the rules that determined whether a person was deemed worthy of God's blessing. Jesus, while firmly within that circle of worthiness, preferred to hang out on the fringes where he could invite those standing outside in – ever expanding the reach of inclusion into God's family.

Spirituality, in general, and Christianity, specifically, calls for an ever-increasing circle of invitation and inclusion. Inclusion is what love requires, even when those we include create discomfort, and even when we may not approve of the lifestyles, beliefs, or practices we allow in. Whenever we question if someone is worthy of inclusion into our family circle we should ask,

Who would Jesus exclude?

"Who would Jesus exclude?" The answer is that Jesus did not exclude anyone. We also need to remember the "circle" does not belong to us, anyway. The circle belongs to God, and it is only by God's grace that we are included within it. Whenever our reading of scripture leads us to exclude, we should read more carefully Jesus' examples of inclusion. Otherwise, we risk creating a spiritual black hole where the mass of our being collapses into itself. No love will enter and no light will escape. The universe God created is expanding its reach. Are we expanding with it?

20. Worshiping ≠ Following

Whoever serves me must follow me, and where I am, there my servant will be also. John 12:26

Twenty-one times in the four Gospels, Jesus says, "Follow me." Clearly, Jesus desired followers. In order to follow, we must commit to two types of action, especially when the leader is not physically present. First, the follower must learn the values and priorities of the one he or she professes to follow. Second, the follower must actually act in ways that are consistent with the priorities of the leader.

In the case of Christians, sometimes we confuse *following* Jesus with *worshiping* Jesus. Do you know how many times in the Bible that Jesus directs us to worship him? Zero. Follow me = 21; worship me = 0. Therefore, worshiping ≠ following. I find this bit of math interesting and telling.

> *Our churches need to be more than just houses of worship.*

Jesus does mention the importance of worshiping the Father throughout the Gospels, but never once says we should worship *him*. Jesus apparently was more interested in our actions on his behalf than in our praise. Jesus spelled out a mission and vision for life that he wanted to outlive his days on earth. It had nothing to do with enhancing his personal glory; but it had everything to do with tending to and expanding his flock.

I believe this tells me that going to church on Sunday mornings – an act of worship – is not sufficient to claim myself as a follower of Jesus. I am not saying that attending worship does not have value or that it cannot help us grow as followers of Christ. Worshiping is not enough, however, at least not by itself. A good church can help us understand what was important to Jesus, but it is up to us to act on that knowledge. Some of the most spiritual, Christ-following people I know choose not to attend church on a regular basis. If going to church on Sunday mornings does not motivate us to follow Jesus into our world, we may be missing the point. We might as well stay home. I believe our churches need to be more than houses of worship. They also need to provide an inspirational call to action to make our world a better place for everyone within it.

To worship is to revere, adore, or pay homage to someone. For many of us, worshiping is primarily an intellectual, non-self-sacrificing act, and that is not good enough for Jesus. Jesus wants our mind, yes, but not without our heart and body. A mind can think great thoughts and still accomplish nothing of value. A mind that guides the work of the heart and body into the world can accomplish great things. Jesus called for human *verbs*, not nouns – he was faith in action, and *acts* of faith are what he seeks from us.

21. The Enemy is Within

Jesus, full of the Holy Spirit, returned from the Jordan and was led by the Spirit in the wilderness, where for forty days he was tempted by the devil. Luke 4:1-2

When I was growing up, there was a popular comedian named Flip Wilson. He would do something he knew he should not do and say, "The devil made me do it!" It was funny because everyone knew it was his own lack of self-control that was to blame. Today, there is significant disagreement about whether the devil is an actual being with power to lead us to evil acts. Because I have not had personal experience with a power outside of myself encouraging me towards evil, I tend to believe there is no such separate entity. I believe we use the devil as an excuse for something within us that we are unwilling to acknowledge, like Flip Wilson, or we blame the devil for something external to us that we do not

> *The source of all evil is the misguided perception by individuals that we are separate, independent beings.*

understand. Having said that, I know people who feel they have had an encounter with an outside, evil spirit, and I respect their perspective.

The issue at hand is not whether there is evil in the world, but where that evil originates. I am not so naïve as to believe there is no evil in the world, but where does our evil enemy actually reside? Do evil acts come from people who are selfish, ignorant, or whose motives are malicious, or do they originate from some external, spiritual being bent on our destruction? Clearly, I lean towards the former explanation. The latter simply gives us an excuse to let ourselves off the hook when our behavior does not line up with expectations.

I believe the source of *all* evil – the birthplace of every enemy – is the misguided perception *by individuals* that we are separate, independent beings. Once we learn to recognize and honor our absolute interconnectedness with others, we will have no enemies – only reflections of our own internal conflicts. There will always be those who do not have our best interests at heart, but we will recognize them for what they are – immature, narcissistic, and misguided. They are fellow humans fighting their own internal demons, not necessarily evil incarnate. They need understanding and help (and sometimes avoidance), not hatred and scorn.

Our sense of an enemy stems from our lack of understanding of the significance of the other. We fear who and what we do not understand. As we begin to realize that what we see external to ourselves is largely a mirror reflecting our internal struggles and unfinished business, we begin to accept responsibility for our part in the evil that manifests in our world. We are connected to all that is, and all that is is connected to us – intimately and securely. The good news is that we can do something to change our external world by changing our internal world. The bad news is that wherever we go, our enemy goes with us.

22. Resurrection is a Reoccurring Reality

Very truly, I tell you, unless a grain of wheat falls into the earth and dies, it remains just a single grain; but if it dies, it bears much fruit. John 12:24

I do not know how I missed it, but resurrection is all around us, all of the time. To be sure, it is called by different names – the changing seasons, graduations, marriages, childbirth, death, sunrise, sunset – but the changing from one phase of life to another is constant. The cycle of birth, growth, death, and rebirth is forever present within us physically, emotionally, and spiritually.

As a Christian, I associate resurrection with the death and resurrection of Jesus Christ. What I missed, however, was that the same pattern is repeated in all of life as a natural, on-going process, albeit not always in such a dramatic fashion. The resurrection of Jesus is a core belief of Christianity, and the resurrection – having its central figure return to life from death – is the distinguishing feature separating it from other enduring religions.

Among Christians, we debate about how much of the biblical record we believe *literally,* but we tend to overlook how much of the lives recorded therein serve as a metaphor

> *Science confirms that rebirth is an on-going process.*

for our lives and the life around us. Science confirms that rebirth is an on-going process. Every cell in our bodies is replaced at least every seven years, so we are entirely remade many times over the course of a lifetime. Jesus talks about wheat in the passage from John 12. He says unless a grain of wheat falls into the ground and "dies," it will forever remain only a single grain of wheat. Once the seed dies, however, it grows into a plant that forms a seed head with hundreds of grains of wheat. When those grains fall to the earth and die, thousands of grains of wheat result. Knowing that, did the initial grain of wheat die, or did it *transform* and expand its existence? Clearly, it was transformed, and so are we whenever a part of us dies. When Jesus rose from the dead, he was not the same person in the same body. He had been transformed. Even his own disciples did not recognize him until he spoke.

The moral of resurrection is that change is good and necessary. New life cannot begin until an old life passes away. This is rebirth, and death is its prerequisite. It is what provides second chances and new starts. Much as we may feel safe and secure in our current life, nothing remains the same for long. We are designed for change, and we are led into numerous transformations over the course of a lifetime. We can change willingly, or we can go kicking and screaming. Either way, we will die to our old self and be reborn to a new one.

23. Unity ≠ Uniformity

The glory that you have given me I have given them, so that they may be one, as we are one. I in them and you in me, that they may become completely one, so that the world may know that you have sent me and have loved them even as you have loved me.
John 17:22-23

As a young adult, I was fascinated with Eastern philosophy. A common theme was *unity,* or *oneness.* Writers spoke frequently of becoming *one* with God, or with one's environment, or with others. In marriage, scripture tells us two lives become *one* flesh (Genesis 2:24). In my western mind, I thought the whole concept of oneness was repulsive. Why would a single drop of water intentionally fall in the ocean and lose its uniqueness? I remember reading once, about marriage, that the ultimate result of two people becoming one was two half-people. Cynical, yes, but it is a reflection of the western emphasis on individuality, making one's own way, and expressing one's distinctiveness.

Interestingly, the point in my life when I was ready to enter into marriage was the point at which I had grown tired of my individual expression. I did not like what I had and had not achieved in life, I felt stagnant

> *Unity is about fitting one's uniqueness into place along with the distinct qualities of others to create something greater.*

and stuck, and I was more than ready to give up the life I had worked to build for a chance of reaching for something better. Marriage changed my life in wonderful ways too numerous to count, but it hardly stole my uniqueness. Rather, unity in marriage provided a larger context of support where I could develop and express my individual gifts more completely. And that is the point about unity that is often overlooked: unity does not equate to uniformity. Unity is about fitting one's uniqueness into place along with the distinct qualities of others to create something greater. Think of the pieces of a puzzle – each piece has a unique coloration, shape, and place, but when the pieces are fit together as one, the result is far beyond what any one piece was capable of producing.

Striving for unity requires a leap of faith. A person must be willing to risk the self they have identified with in order to attain a larger purpose or goal. The math of unity is $1+1+1=111$. There is very little logic to it, but we know two or more people working in unison toward a common purpose can accomplish more than can be accomplished individually. The power of relationship is the immeasurable wildcard. Jesus said, "For where two or three are gathered in my name, I am there among them." (Matthew 18:20) It is an early expression of fellowship, and it implies that a supernatural force develops from oneness.

Every trait that made me unique in my single days – good and not-so-good – I retain today, so I lost nothing. Instead, I found a greater context within which to express that uniqueness.

24. Faith is a Good Start

Then the king will say to those at his right hand, "Come, you that are blessed by my Father, inherit the kingdom prepared for you from the foundation of the world; for I was hungry and you gave me food, I was thirsty and you gave me something to drink, I was a stranger and you welcomed me, I was naked and you gave me clothing, I was sick and you took care of me, I was in prison and you visited me." Truly I tell you, just as you did it to one of the least of these who are members of my family, you did it to me.
Matthew 25:34-36, 40

Religious circles emphasize the importance of faith. Faith is the belief in something beyond what we can see or fully understand. It provides a broader vision than our eyes can see and a more sensitive hearing than is possible from our ears alone. Faith acknowledges that for all we know and for all the information we have available to us, there is much that is and will always remain a mystery. Religious faith acknowledges a higher, benevolent power that assures all things work together for good. Christians name that power God.

I believe developing a faith in something larger than ourselves and in purposes greater than our circle of interest is important for our individual and collective development, regardless of whether that faith is a *religious* faith, and regardless of whether we express that faith in a church. Developing faith is a practical way to live. Jesus, in Matthew 17, says that faith the size of a mustard seed can move mountains. The implication is that a small amount of faith can increase whatever power is available in order to overcome tremendous challenges.

Faith is a multiplier. We can accomplish more with faith in something beyond ourselves than we can accomplish alone. I want to emphasize the word *accomplish*. One purpose for the gift of faith is to accomplish *something*. Not that faith, alone, is not worthwhile. The apostle Paul says we are "justified" by

> *Developing a faith in something larger than ourselves and in purposes greater than our circle of interest is important for our development.*

faith, or made right with God. That we establish a faith connection with a higher, benevolent power is one thing. We might even worship that power on Sunday mornings, but are we using the power of that faith to accomplish something for the greater good? God's power unites with ours, through faith, in order to co-create a better world. I believe faith should inspire us to work for justice, to feed the hungry, to welcome strangers, and to house the homeless. Jesus modeled a life-giving faith and dedicated himself to meeting the needs of a broken world. He valued his time with his Father, going away from the crowds frequently to pray, but he used that connection to renew his ability to serve. The faith of Jesus is an active, achieving faith, and that type of faith leaves a positive imprint.

The writer of James proclaims that faith without works is dead (James 2:17). The Bible is full of stories of ordinary people who responded in faith and accomplished extraordinary things. Why would we believe we are capable of anything less? Our faith is a wonderful thing, but our faith calls us to greater things. True faith inspires and empowers us to make good things happen in our world.

25. Truth is Paradoxical

Those who believe in me, even though they die, will live, and everyone who lives and believes in me will never die.
John 11:25c-26a

A paradox is something that seems contradictory to popular opinion or common sense. The good news is that paradoxical reasoning does not trouble most of us too often. The bad news is that it probably should. The Bible is full of paradoxical bits of wisdom – nonsensical statements that seemingly contradict themselves. Jesus was a king of paradox. Here is a sampling:

"But many who are first will be last, and the last will be first." (Mark 10:31)
"Those who find their life will lose it, and those who lose their life for my sake will find it." (Matthew 10:39)

"Those who try to make their life secure will lose it, but those who lose their life will keep it." (Luke 17:33)

Jesus taught with stories, or parables, few of which gave clear answers and many defied common sense. What Jesus understood about truth is that it is inherently paradoxical, and that is a constant obstacle for many of us. Much of what we hold to be true is actually only partially true, or at least not entirely true. We separate light and dark for our own understanding, but they are actually manifestations of the same reality. We cannot know darkness without first knowing light, and darkness is simply the absence of light. Other examples of single realities include bliss and sorrow, life and death, right and wrong, good and evil, happy and sad. Each is defined by the other, and neither can be known except in relation to the other. They are two ends of a single continuum, but we treat them as distinct realities. We try our best to be

> *Our entire existence is held together by a tension of opposites that characterizes every aspect of our lives.*

good and are disappointed when we act in not-so-good ways. What we thought to be right turns out to be wrong in another circumstance. What we assumed to be virtuous turns out to be evil from another vantage point. When our sports team wins a game we are excited; but our thrill comes at the expense of fans of the other team who may be devastated. The game is a single reality experienced from two different points of view – one positive and one negative. In his book, *Yes, And,…*, Fr. Richard Rohr[7] writes, "You and I are living paradoxes, which everybody can see except us."

Our entire existence is held together by a *tension of opposites* that characterizes every aspect of our lives. It is nearly impossible for us to reconcile these opposites in a meaningful, understandable way. And therein lies the key to dealing with mysterious realities – we cannot reconcile the paradox. Our challenge is not to solve the mystery but to *transcend* the seeming enigma and *transform* our experience and understanding of it.

Chief among the paradoxes we must transcend is our understanding of life and death. Death is an inextricable part of life. Death does not mean the *end* of life but a new beginning. In his cryptic way, when Jesus tells us we must die in order to *live*, he is not referring to our physical death. Jesus is speaking of a transformation of our life into one consistent with his. We are not asked to give up our life, physically, but to enter into a new version of that life which transforms our former existence to a new one. We cannot understand Jesus' teachings about new life with our traditional understanding of life and death. It is a paradox – an irreconcilable enigma – when seen through our old eyes. Life is more than we can see, hear, feel, and touch with our earthly senses. As we learn to engage our spiritual senses, the formerly paradoxical becomes perfectly acceptable, if not always understandable.

26. Prayer is a Way of Life

Rejoice always, pray without ceasing, give thanks in all circumstances; for this is the will of God in Christ Jesus for you.
1 Thessalonians 5:16-17
Likewise the Spirit helps us in our weakness, for we do not know how to pray as we ought."
Romans 8:26

For most of my life, prayer occurred at a specified time or event, or else it was something I carved out a special time for from the rest of my day. It was how I was taught. We prayed before meals, head bowed and hands folded; at bedtime, kneeling at the edge of my bed; and during church. Most prayers were recited by rote, saying the same words each time. It seemed more like a redundant formality than an expression of sincere need or gratitude.

As I got older, my prayers became more conversational. Particularly in my bachelor days when I spent large swaths of time alone, I found myself in conversations with God. Most of the time it was a one-way conversation – I talked and assumed God was listening. There were times, however, I believe God answered. God's answers did not come as spoken responses, however, nor did they arrive according to my expected timeline. Rather, they came at unpredictable times as an inspiration or an intuition that helped me see an issue in a new way. Answers came with expansions of my awareness, making me believe the reason I could not hear God earlier was because I prejudged the answer. In other words, if God did not seem to answer, the problem was not because God did not answer, but because God answered in a way I was not ready or capable to accept. Like most stumbling blocks in my life, the problem within myself had to first be identified and resolved.

Paul's exhortation in his first letter to the Thessalonians to "pray without ceasing" seemed ridiculous. How could anyone devote his or her entire life to praying? As long as prayer is an interruption to one's day, there can be no simultaneous living and praying, at least not on a regular, sustainable basis. A clue to the resolution of this dilemma is found in Paul's letter to the Romans, "...we do not know how to pray as we ought." The challenge is not that we must take more time out of our day to pray; rather, we must find ways to live our days in a more prayerful manner.

> *As long as prayer is an interruption to one's day, there can be no simultaneous living and praying.*

For most of my life, I used prayer judiciously. After all, I did not want to draw too much divine attention to some of what I did. When I was in trouble, when I was sad, when I was lost or broken, I would turn to God in prayer. God, however, does not want to *only* be our God in our times of difficulty. I believe God experiences creation *through* us, meaning God experiences creation *with* us. Assuming that is the case, why would God only want to experience the difficult times? If our good times consist of actions we feel God would not want to experience with us, we need either rethink our actions or rethink our understanding of the interests of God.

Sin is that which separates us from God and others. If God wishes to experience life with and through us, our sin keeps that from happening. It is not that sin prevents God from experiencing with and through us, but our sin prevents *us* from experiencing God experiencing with and through us. In other words, we suffer twice – first from the separation caused by our sin, and second by not being consciously aware of our communion with the accepting, encouraging presence of God. Emmanuel, God with us, is not something that happens when we become holier. Emmanuel has been with us since before our birth. Prayer is communion *with* God. In order to experience God in a conscious way, we must keep ourselves in the ever-flowing rhythm of the divine and, thus, aware of God's constant presence. In the process, our entire life becomes one unceasing prayer.

27. Growth is not Chronological

But do not ignore this one fact, beloved, that with the Lord one day is like a thousand years, and a thousand years are like one day.
2 Peter 3:8

Beginning at birth, our bodies go through a mostly predictable cycle of growth, maturation, decline, and death. We see it in others, and most of us witness it firsthand in ourselves. Through our school years, we steadily advance in our academic achievements as we graduate from grade to grade. As such, it is only natural to expect our growth as spiritual beings to follow a similar, regular pattern; but it does not. Our experience of time is very different from that of God. In other words, time is not always as it seems. Our human evolution seemingly progresses in a predictable manner from past to present to future. God creates, and that creation – including our lives – manifests in ways that we can only experience gradually over time. That is not necessarily the core reality, however.

Because our spiritual growth – our increasing awareness of *God with us* – occurs outside of earth-time, our spiritual development seems to occur in fits and starts. We go through long periods where it seems nothing is changing. In fact, we go through periods where it seems we are falling back and losing what we once believed we had attained. Then something happens and we hardly recognize the person we were a short time earlier. Our spiritual growth is commonly experienced as three steps forward and two steps back.

Often painfully, the times we leap forward in a spiritual way are the times that force us to reevaluate our understanding of the world. The single event that most contributed to my spiritual development was the sudden death of my father when I was a youth. Decades later, that experience continues to realign my understandings and priorities. For others it may be a serious accident or illness, a divorce, or the severe misfortune of someone close to them that drives their former certainties into a state of utter inadequacy. In physical development, athletic trainers tell us, "No pain, no gain." The same is often true in our spiritual growth. We grow too fond of the status quo when life is too comfortable. God created our world, including us, to evolve. When we are not changing, we are

> *Our spiritual development seems to occur in fits and starts.*

not growing. Sometimes, we only need a slight nudge to move; other times, we need a swift kick in the back side.

We know our experience of chronological time is variable at best. When we are absorbed in a task we enjoy, time flies by. When we are burdened with a dreadful job, however, the clock hardly seems to move. In childhood, time moved at a crawl. As we age, the days in a month and months in a year seem fewer and fewer. Author Gretchen Rubin[8] said, "The days are long, but the years are short." Truly, even time is not the stable foundation we assume.

Our growth as human and spiritual beings does not correspond to our calendar because spiritual and physical times do not always correspond. Why does this matter? It matters because we are often too hard on others and on ourselves based on appearances on any given day. God's creation, including us, is good. From our perspective, we are always a work in progress. From God's perspective, we are the image of God; and in God's present, we are *very good!* We simply do not have eyes to see it (yet). That knowledge can and will transform our world.

28. Tithing is not Enough

But woe to you Pharisees! For you tithe mint and rue and herbs of all kinds, and neglect justice and the love of God; it is these you ought to have practiced, without neglecting the others. Luke 11:42

Of all the expectations placed on the churchgoers among us, few cause as much discomfort and difference of opinion as the obligation to financially support our houses of worship. *Tithes and offerings* are spoken of regularly in both Old and New Testaments, although the expectation to tithe is more explicit in the Old. A *tithe* means a tenth; thus, the common understanding that we are to give a tenth of our income in support of our church.

> *Jesus wanted followers who willingly and happily gave everything.*

In previous generations, that may have been clear-cut, but not anymore. Are we to tithe on our *gross* or our *net* income? Do donations to other worthy causes count as part of our tithe? If we have an unusual expense one year, can the "tenth" be reduced? If we find $20.00 lying in the street, must we tithe on that, too?

In early Jewish history, the Levites, one of the 12 tribes of Israel, were designated as the keepers of the Temple. Because their livelihood was the business of the Temple, they could not make a living in other ways. The Levites were dependent on the tithes of the people from other tribes for their support. The concept remains in place today, with members of a church providing financial support to pay the salaries of the staff and expenses of the church. Often overlooked is that the Biblical expectation for giving went well beyond the tithe. Separate *offerings* were also requested at various times, and those offerings could add another ten to twenty percent of income or wealth on top of the tithe. Today, I believe the percent of income given by the average church member is about 2%. Five percent is considered generous, although a tithe is still held out as the standard.

Jesus, however, held a much different measure for giving. He did not request a simple tithe; he wanted followers who willingly and happily gave *everything*. A rich man (Mark 10:17-22) tells Jesus he has followed every commandment and asks what else he must do to enter the kingdom of heaven. Jesus tells him to sell everything he has and give it to the poor. The man walks away, disappointed, for he was not willing to give up his many possessions. In a parable found in Matthew 13:44, Jesus tells of a field with treasure such that someone *desires* to sell everything he or she owns in return for that one field. In the next verse, he tells of a pearl of great value such that one *desires* to sell everything else in order to obtain. For Jesus, the important matter is not how much we have or give, but of where our heart is – what do we most desire? Do we prefer our "stuff" to the life Jesus offers? The treasure-filled field and the pearl of great value represent the kingdom he encourages us to seek. When our heart is in the right place, nothing else will matter.

Far be it from me to imply churches are the only organizations worthy of financial support. Actually, I think that line of reasoning misses the point. Where is our heart? Where is our desire? Tithing – supporting our houses of worship – is a good start, but it is not enough. The key is to find ways to make every act of every day an *offering* for God to use for good. Whether we are eating, exercising, playing, getting ready for bed, or working, we are encouraged to offer everything for God's purposes. Whatever we do, our actions and decisions impact others. Making our life an offering is recognizing that God is with us all the time, in every circumstance, whether we want or sense God there or not. God will not be locked in a church but is an active presence in our lives, no matter how mundane or profane some of our moments may be. Jesus reminds us in the Gospel of Luke that we cannot neglect justice or love. Jesus tells us when we willingly dedicate our heart and life to following him, the rest will fall into place. It is not that where our money goes is unimportant, but it is more important to examine the desire of our heart. "For where your treasure is, there your heart will be also" (Matthew 6:21).

29. The Language of God is Silence

Be still, and know that I am God!
Psalm 46:10a

Words encapsulate and narrow our lives. If we are not talking to someone, our internal dialogue is running rampant. If we are not interrupting the speaker, we are planning how to respond, instead of listening with a mind open to learning something new. After we converse with another person, we often replay and analyze the dialogue. We may think of things we wish we had or had not said, or we may wonder what the other person meant by words they used or how they spoke them. The point is that immediately after an experience, we begin reshaping the experience with our words. The actual experience ends and the less-than-accurate description of the experience takes its place.

Words are symbols for things, not the things themselves. We describe, label, and categorize, but words themselves have no substance. We might describe a picture in detail, but the image in the hearer's mind will still be very different from the actual picture. Such is the nature of a verbal description – it is not the reality. Our words always remove us a step or more from the experience. Thus, the biblical directive to "Be still."

The early Jewish people did not believe the name of God should be spoken. When Moses met God at the burning bush, he asked God for a name to give the people. God said, "*I am who I am*" (Exodus 3:14). Once we have named something, we narrow our belief about its nature. If we say, "This is a maple tree," we believe it is

> *We describe, label, and categorize, but words themselves have no substance.*

not a rock or a person. As soon as we begin describing God with words, we limit the possibilities of an otherwise limitless God. Our tendency toward naming and describing makes it easier for us to understand and process our experiences, but as our words remove us from those experiences, we trade the words for the reality. Much beauty, depth, and meaning is forever lost in the process.

The Psalmist encourages us to still our minds. There are many ways to do this, all of which require focus and persistence. Yoga, meditation, centering or contemplative prayer are a few ways to silence our inner dialogue long enough to draw closer to God. God's language appears silent to us because God does not speak as we do. In the creation story, God *speaks* the world into being. "Then God *said*, 'Let there be light,' and there was light." (Genesis 1:3) God's voice itself provided the creative power. Similarly, in the first chapter of John, the *Word* of God became flesh in Jesus. God's creative language does not interface with our spoken language, and we cannot *experience* it as long as our internal dialogue interrupts and interprets. As the Psalmist says, we must "be still" to know God.

30. Prophesy is About the Present

For they are a rebellious people, faithless children, children who will not hear the instruction of the Lord; who say to the seers, "Do not see"; and to the prophets, "Do not prophesy to us what is right; speak to us smooth things, prophesy illusions, leave the way, turn aside from the path, let us hear no more about the Holy One of Israel." Isaiah 30:9-12

My understanding of prophesy was always of something future-oriented, as in predicting the future. My scant readings of biblical prophecy did nothing to correct my ignorance. Last fall, I heard Sister Audrey Doetzel[9] explain that prophesy is "courageously telling the present," and her insights opened my eyes to the vital purpose and tenuous place of prophets throughout history. In biblical times, and still today, prophets lived in a space described by Fr. Richard Rohr and others as the "edge of the inside." They live as part of the current culture, but they remain on the fringes of society. From

> *A prophesy is a reading of the present situation, even when it points to a future calamity.*

there, they observe and participate in the here and now, while retaining a distance that allows for a unique and broader perspective.

The prophets of the Old Testament were often servants of rulers whose job it was to read the signs of the times. When their reading proved incorrect or unpopular, they sometimes were put to death. Some of those prophesies were future-oriented, as in "If you continue on this path, this (bad thing) will happen." A prophesy, however, is a reading of the *present* situation, even when it points to a future calamity. Common to prophets then and now, however, is that prophets speak *truth to power*. Prophets almost exclusively speak on behalf of the disadvantaged to the advantaged.

Artists, poets, authors, and songwriters are often the prophets of the day, holding up a mirror to society, saying, "Look at what you have become." The message of the prophets throughout time has not always been welcomed or received kindly. Jesus, himself, testified that a prophet has no honor in the prophet's own country (John 4:44). The 1960's saw an explosion of contemporary prophets, including Bob Dylan[10]:

> *Come gather 'round people wherever you roam, And admit that the waters around you have grown;*
> *Accept it that soon you'll be drenched to the bone, If your time to you is worth savin',*
> *Then you better start swimmin', or you'll sink like a stone, For the times, they are a-changin'.*

And Paul Simon[11]:

> *And the people bowed and prayed, to the neon god they made;*
> *And the sign flashed out its warning, in the words that it was forming,*
> *And the sign said, "The words of the prophets are written on the subway walls*
> *And tenement halls," And whispered in the sounds of silence.*

Those railing against the status quo welcomed these and other artists in the 1960's, but they were threats to the established order. They gave a voice to those who felt they had none. Unsettled times bring prophets to the forefront where their perspective is needed, if not always applauded. Sister Audrey[9], quoting Thomas Moore, said prophesy is "an ethical motivation that leads to criticism of, or at least an alternative to, *a highly narcissistic and materialistic culture* (emphasis added)." She describes the 21st century prophets' call as one to make "the invisible God audible and visible." I agree wholeheartedly, and there can be no more timely need than now for ethical prophesies of that sort. The questions are: "Who will speak truth to power today?" and, once heard, "Who will act upon it?"

It is important to beware of false prophets, however. Jesus issued his warning in Matthew 7:15, "Beware of false prophets, who come to you in sheep's clothing but inwardly are ravenous wolves. You will know them by their fruits." In assessing would-be prophets, it is wise to ask, "What do they hunger for?" My sense is that today's political partisans, on both sides, are closer to the powerful, ravenous wolf than to the sheep. If a person or group hungers for power or for the degradation or destruction of others, it cannot be the all-inclusive God they are making audible.

31. Salvation is Communal

For as in one body we have many members, and not all the members have the same function, so we, who are many, are one body in Christ, and individually we are members one of another.
Romans 12:4

One thing I despised in college was group assignments. The instructor would assign several students a task and, together, they had to complete and present the assignment as a team. Every member received the same grade, regardless of how much or little he or she contributed to the final product. Being fiercely independent, I wanted to succeed or fail alone and did *not* want my grade to be dependent on others.

My father was in the Army Air Force during World War II, and although he was not a part of the D Day invasion of France, I reflect on that action as if he were. The Normandy invasion was needed in order to break the German stronghold along the English Channel so the Allies could liberate France and, eventually, the rest of Europe. The problem was the concrete, machine-gun bunkers lined along the Channel. The Allies knew it would take a concentration of sustained force to break open a line in the German defenses so troops could enter and eventually drive the Nazis out of France. They also knew many lives would be lost. Of the 24,000 men landing on Normandy that morning, nearly half were killed or wounded. There were similar numbers of German casualties. It was a bloodbath on all sides. Many individual lives were required to join together to accomplish a single goal. Thousands of those individuals – sons, brothers, and fathers – willingly served as *bullet recipients* so those behind them could eventually destroy and advance beyond the machine-gun bunkers.

The Bible seldom speaks of individual salvation. Salvation – the freeing and advancing to higher levels of existence – is communal in that its attainment is for the benefit of a group. The Hebrew people were saved, collectively, from their oppression in Egypt. Noah's extended family was saved from the great flood. Organizations succeed when its members move together in the same direction. Marriages flourish when the union prospers both partners. Individual effort is required, but to accomplish great things requires many individuals working together toward a common goal.

Paul, in a number of his letters, describes believers as a single body, with each member having a specific function. All members work together and are necessary for *the good of the body.* Jesus' comment that there is no greater love than to lay down one's life for another (John 15:13) is an expression of the willing subjugation of individual interests for the sake of something greater. Appearances aside, we are all members of a single body.

> *The Bible seldom speaks of individual salvation.*

I sometimes act as if I were self-made person, that whatever I have achieved has been by my effort alone. It is a self-deception of enormous proportion. When we fail to acknowledge others for what we accomplish together, when we believe our personal objectives outweigh those of the larger community, we may be prone to believe we can attain salvation alone. Could my right hand separate itself from the rest of my body and prosper? What sort of salvation do we think we will attain, a paradise of one? That sounds more like solitary confinement. No, life is a group project, a family undertaking, one body with all its parts working in harmony. In spite of what we may choose to believe, we sink or swim, pass or fail, together. We will succeed when our personal goals, desires, and actions are in accord with those of the greater family to which we belong. Too often we ask, "What do *I* need to do to get to heaven?" instead of focusing on what is required to manifest heaven on earth – not just for me, but also for everyone; and not just for some distant future, but also for today.

32. Mercy Trumps Justice

He has told you, O mortal, what is good; and what does the Lord require of you but to do justice, and to love kindness, and to walk humbly with your God? Micah 6:8

If a starving person is offered a meal or a job, and they can only choose one, which will he or she accept? Would we judge them as lazy if they took the meal over the job? Would we judge them as less hungry than they claimed if they took the job? My guess is that a truly hungry person would *always* choose the meal – not because they are lazy and do not want a job, but because they are *hungry,* and satisfying their hunger is their most immediate need.

In this example, providing a meal is an act of mercy; providing a job is an act of justice. Mercy addresses an immediate physical, emotional, or spiritual need, where justice works toward a longer-term solution to the need. The cruelty of this example, and all too common in reality, is that a person in need is forced to choose between two important blessings, *both* of which are necessary. The challenge for us as individuals and as a society is how best to provide both. Time management professionals suggest separating our daily tasks into those that are important and those that are urgent. Urgent tasks must be done first because they are, well, urgent. Important tasks must be completed, but not necessarily today. Important tasks that are not addressed within a reasonable time, however, become urgent. It is easy for us to become so consumed with urgent tasks, including those that are not important, that we leave insufficient time for the important but non-urgent issues. In this time management context, mercy is urgent and justice is important.

In his bestselling and insightful book, *When Breath Becomes Air,* Paul Kalanithi[12] writes, "There is a tension in the Bible between justice and mercy...The main message of Jesus, I believe, is that mercy trumps justice every time." When there is an urgent need, mercy is required.

> *Mercy addresses an immediate need, where justice works toward a longer-term solution.*

For this reason, we quickly send needed resources to the sites of natural and man-made disasters. Although mercy may trump justice in the immediate future, justice cannot be ignored if one is to be freed from the on-going need for mercy. This is our dilemma in helping the needy. There are many immediate needs for mercy: food, clothing, and shelter; but there are equally important needs for justice: good jobs, quality healthcare, affordable housing, accessible childcare, and legal protection from discrimination. Of course, works of mercy and justice both require funding, and those funds are increasingly difficult to generate.

Jesus recognized that mercy comes first. A hungry crowd cannot hear even the most profound sermon, so he made sure his followers had something to eat in addition to something to learn. We can model Jesus' example. When a person is not receiving a blessing we are trying to impart, perhaps we should ask what is standing between him or her and the blessing. Are they hungry? Are they addicted to something that draws their attention away? Are they safe? Are they in physical or emotional distress? It is possible for our best, most sincere efforts at establishing justice to fail when we do not first recognize and attend to the more immediate needs for mercy. Likewise, it is possible for our lack of focus on justice to result in our resources being consumed by a never-ending cycle of need for mercy. There is a delicate balance to establish between the two. Our challenge is to find that balance, beginning with mercy.

33. Anger is a Secondary Emotion

Be angry, but do not sin; do not let the sun go down on your anger.
Ephesians 4:26

There are too many times on too many days that I experience anger. Sometimes, it is my own anger; other times, I am the target of the anger of another. Anger crops up at work, at home, in traffic, in politics, and yes, even at church. Some people are quick to get angry, but then calm down in short order. I am the opposite. Usually, it takes quite a lot to arouse my anger and, once angry, I can stew for days or weeks.

Our anger, however, is not a primary emotion. Although anger commands a lot of attention, it always masks something else. We may consider someone an *angry person,* but he or she is more likely a person whose anger is stimulated easily, quickly, and often. If we want to get to the heart of anger – ours or that of another – we must look deeper. It starts with an event that we interpret as threatening. It is the threat, real or perceived, that generates the anger. Once we are angry, any number of consequences may ensue, many of them unpleasant. To effectively deal with anger, we must first identify the

> *Relationships are fertile ground for anger because no strong relationship is possible without shared vulnerability.*

threat preceding it and understand why it triggers such feelings of vulnerability. In identifying and examining the threat, we may realize we have exaggerated the risk, often to the point of absurdity. For example, when someone cuts us off in traffic, we may lay on our horn and yell, "What are you trying to do, kill me?" The triggering event is the car pulling in front of us, the threat is our perceived imminent death at the hands of a homicidal maniac, and the result is anger.

Anger, once aroused, can lead to acts of verbal, emotional, or physical violence, and therein lies the problem. Many everyday events threaten us. When we examine the event and our initial reaction to it we can recognize our fear, humiliation, indignation, annoyance, or any of many emotional responses, and we can begin to understand that none of these events *require* us to become angry. The anger, the secondary emotion, is a choice, albeit often an unconscious and unhelpful one. The challenge is to become consciously aware enough to allow ourselves to *decide* whether to react in anger. Too often, our anger bursts out uninvited, leaving a mess we immediately regret.

Relationships are fertile ground for anger because no strong relationship is possible without a willing and shared vulnerability. What would not be a triggering event in other circumstances can lead to an emotional explosion between people in close, regular proximity to each other. A dish not rinsed before going into the dishwasher, dirty clothes left on the floor, a car left nearly empty of fuel – all can leave us feeling unappreciated, belittled, or invisible. If we are not intentional and measured in our response, anger may ensue.

The challenge for me, as with most of the choices I make, is to take the time to assess my reactions to the countless stimuli around me. Why do certain things threaten me so? What am I afraid of? Will this matter a year from now? How does this compare to the challenges faced by those in third-world countries, or to the parent whose child has cancer? I find perspective helpful when analyzing emotions, just as analyzing the triggering events and my initial responses are helpful in exploring my anger. When I am the object of someone else's anger, it is sometimes helpful to ponder, "What have I done that this person perceives as threatening?" Writing him or her off as just an angry, unpleasant person is not helpful or instructive – something is hurting them. Questions like these help me accept responsibility for the anger around me, which is important because I cannot improve a situation until I accept at least some responsibility for its creation.

34. We are to Become Christ-Like

Very truly I tell you, the one who believes in me will also do the works that I do and, in fact, will do greater works than these, because I am going to the Father. John 14:12

Author, teacher, and speaker Fr. Richard Rohr often writes that *Christ* is not Jesus' last name. Christ is a designation for one in whom spirit and body are perfectly integrated and manifested. Christ consciousness is a state of being that has existed as part of the Godhead since the beginning of creation. Jesus was 100% human and 100% God – a perfect expression of body and spirit, and he invites us to become the same. His oft-repeated mandate, "Follow me," does not mean to go where he went, but to become who he was – to do what he did, to love as he loved, and to heal as he healed. How did I miss that?

I find ample evidence to justify that Jesus encouraged us to fully develop our spiritual natures, even as we develop our human nature. For example, beginning with John 17:20, "I ask not only on behalf of these *(his disciples)*, but also on behalf of those who will believe in me through their word *(that's us)*, that they may all be one. As you, Father, are in me and I am in you, may they also be in us…" Those who have come to believe in Jesus through the words of his disciples, i.e., the Gospels, are invited to become one with God, Jesus, and with each other. That proclamation of *oneness* with God is what got Jesus crucified. This invitation to oneness extends to us, as those who came to believe as a result of the disciples.

Whether by teaching or by imagination, I grew up assuming Jesus the Christ was a larger-than-life figure that I could never aspire to imitating. I, after all, believed I was a lowly and unworthy sinner. It is evident to me now that Jesus believed differently. He not only loves us, but he envisions a divine destiny for and with every one of us. He clearly directed his disciples to continue his work, and we are the current day descendants of those disciples.

To imagine becoming one with Christ *while still on earth* is difficult to grasp. Yet, with God all things are possible. Clearly, we underestimate our capability and our possibilities. Science has shown that we only develop a fraction of our intellectual capacity. What portion of our spiritual capacity is ever realized? Likely, it is minuscule. What if we were to abandon what has become the driving forces in our lives –

> *Jesus not only loves us, but he envisions a divine destiny for and with every one of us.*

prestige, possessions, and power – and unwaveringly centered our lives on service to others, as Jesus did? What if we became such pure and empty vessels that Christ could work through us without resistance? Dare we believe we could heal illness with a word or a touch? Dare we believe we could lift the weight of sin from another's shoulders? Dare we believe the limitless possibilities? I think Jesus urges us so to dare.

35. Love is (always) the Answer

This is my commandment, that you love one another as I have loved you. John 15:12

The opposite of love is *not* hate. Hate is an emotion. The opposite of love is *apathy*, or not caring. Love is an action we choose to give or withhold. My friend, Stan Hughes, describes love as caring enough to *do* something. Because love is a verb, when Jesus commands us to love one another, he is telling us to care about others enough to *take action* on their behalf. He says nothing about liking another, or enjoying their company, or feeling that they deserve our care – those are emotions. Jesus tells us to love others as he loved us – unconditionally, sacrificially, and eternally.

There are a number of reasons why loving someone can be difficult. First, love makes us *vulnerable*. When we do something for another, they may not

> *When we are puzzled about what best to do in a given situation, the answer is always more love.*

reciprocate or appreciate our generosity, and then we may feel stupid, cheated, or otherwise taken advantage of. We are to love anyway. Second, loving another can be *expensive* – financially, emotionally, or physically – and we may feel we cannot afford to love. We are to love anyway. Third, committing to love another takes time and attention away from other important activities. We are to love anyway. Our loving attention is life-giving and is sorely needed everywhere.

When we are puzzled about what best to do in a given situation or with another person, the answer is *always* more love. Love, when properly understood and applied, will not lead us astray. Obviously, loving someone does not necessarily mean we do whatever the object of our love asks. The term *tough love* comes to mind, where the loving actions we choose may not be anything the other person interprets as love, at least not at the time. Our actions might even cause him or her pain. There were times, when my children were young, I refused them something they felt they simply *had* to have. Love is not meek, weak, or unaware. For love to be effective, it must be conscious and intentional.

Robert Greenleaf[13], in his essay *The Servant as Leader*, writes that we are to accept "unlimited liability" for others. Even in the business context from which he wrote, Greenleaf believed that leaders should take responsibility for the lives and well-being of those impacted by his or her company, just as a faithful servant would do. A leader committed to serving others will make decisions that consider the effect on his or her employees, customers, shareholders, and community. Accepting unlimited liability means our responsibility for those affected by our actions never ends – love demands that we always care enough to act in what we sincerely believe to be the best interest of those we love.

Ultimately, however, there is a selfish reason to love. In order to love others fully, we must expand our awareness to include their reality. While we do not need to accept their reality as our own, we do need to respect and acknowledge it. In love, we open our minds to be more aware and, in the process, a larger community of others enriches us. We grow closer to the God who is the Divine Parent to everyone; the same God that loves and accepts unlimited liability for all. We grow closer to the One who is the source of love, the One who *is* love. As we become more loving, we become capable of receiving love, and our world becomes a better, healthier, and more pleasant place for everyone. How did I miss that?

Epilogue

The idea to explore a list of truths I missed at times in my life began in the summer of 2016 when I was asked to preach a sermon at my church on a Sunday morning when our senior pastor was out of town. I am not a preacher, so the thought of acting as if I were was uncomfortable. I had been giving a lot of thought to things I had missed, however, so I decided to share them. I feel it is appropriate to share these thoughts again at the end of the book that began with them.

How Did I Miss That?

(A Sermon)

Then Jacob woke from his sleep and said, "Surely the Lord is in this place and I did not know it!" And he was afraid, and said, "How awesome is this place! This is none other than the house of God, and this is the gate of heaven."
Genesis 28:16-17

From that time Jesus began to proclaim, "Repent, for the kingdom of heaven has come near."
Matthew 4:17

I do not know how I missed it. I am tempted to blame my mother and father. It is easy to say the churches I attended over the decades failed in their responsibility to properly educate me. But somewhere in my childhood, and reinforced throughout my life, was the concept that heaven and hell were faraway places where we would go after we die. Heaven was somewhere above, and hell was somewhere below. Heaven was a paradise where we would be reunited with long-dead relatives. It was a place of angels flying about, playing harps, bounding from cloud to cloud with choirs singing, and where there were no problems, sickness, or death. For whatever reason, the images I was taught about heaven evoked images of family reunions with lots of great aunts and uncles talking about wheat prices, the Great Depression, their aches and pains, and how much harder their lives were than mine, and I thought, "Why would I want to spend eternity here?" Hell, on the other hand, was a place of fire and brimstone, of never-ending heat and misery, where we were stuck with other miserable sinners for all of eternity.

I am not certain exactly when it happened. For sure, it was a process of awakening to the fact that heaven and hell may not be what I had been taught. They may or may not be future states we experience when we leave this earth – we cannot know for sure – but clearly they are current states we experience as a part of our lives on earth, here and now. I do not know how I missed it, because it is written many times throughout scripture. For example, in the Genesis scripture above, Jacob has a dream where angels are ascending and descending along a ladder stretching up to heaven from the very place he was sleeping. He wakes up and realizes he is in the house of God and at the gate to heaven – in the very place he was standing on the earth! From the New Testament, the first words Jesus utters as he begins his ministry that the kingdom of heaven is *near*, as recorded in Matthew and repeated many times throughout the Gospels. Even in the Lord's Prayer, which I've recited nearly every Sunday of my life, we say, "Thy kingdom come, thy will be done *on earth*, as it is in heaven." In Luke 9, Jesus says, "But truly I tell you, there are some standing here who will not taste death before they see the kingdom of God." How did I miss that?

I think I missed it because I relied on the folk wisdom developed over time from the Biblical passages, instead of focusing on the spirit of Jesus' words as recorded in the Bible. It is much easier and safer to consider places like heaven and hell when they are somewhere in the (hopefully) distant future. If they are states of the here and now, we may be obligated to do something about it, here and now. We Methodists rely on experience, reason, and tradition to help us interpret scripture, and this is one area where I believe our traditional understandings have led us astray. Both in our beliefs about heaven and hell, as well as our beliefs about eternity.

We have come to consider "eternity" as our state of being after our physical body dies. The fallacy in this belief is that it assumes our physical body and our soul are two separate entities. I believe Jesus was telling us that we are eternal beings that one day will shed this physical shell, just as at the end of a day we shed the clothing we wore for that particular day. In eternal terms, the significance of the two acts may be more similar than they seem. If Jesus taught us anything it is that we have nothing to fear in death. "Let the dead bury their own dead," he said. We are supposed to be about the business of living, regardless of which side of the grave we are on.

Most of us were taught the Christmas version of heaven and hell -- which is a perversion both of the birth of Jesus and of future states of being. If we are good little boys and girls in this life, Santa-God will award us the gift of eternal life in heaven when we die. The problem is, just like at Christmas, we never know exactly how good we have to be. How many transgressions can we afford and still receive our reward? Ten? Five? None? With only two post-death options – heaven or hell – the stakes are very high. In my mind, the uncertainty itself puts us in a hellish state, here and now.

Another dilemma is that we never know when we are going to die. Our traditions have taught us, indeed certain scriptures affirm, that it does not matter when in our earthly lives we accept the gift of eternal life – or come to faith – but what if we wait too long? What if in our final breath we forget to say the *magic* words, or forget what the magic words are? Then what? Because of one momentary lapse, we are doomed to an eternity in hell? I do not think so.

One of my favorite authors, Fr. Richard Rohr[14], writes that "Hell (is)...when life...(becomes) exclusion, blaming, and denying. We no longer need to believe in hell as a doctrine or a geographic place. We see it in this world almost every day."

Understanding heaven and hell as earthly states is easier when we understand the nature and connectedness of faith, sin, and repentance. Faith is the belief in things not seen – trusting there is *more beyond* what our senses detect. Faith is a heart-felt knowing that God will make all things work together for good, even when we cannot see how that is possible. Trusting in God's goodness is a manifestation of faith and a prerequisite to finding heaven in our daily lives. Conversely, a lack of faith puts many of us in a state of hell day after day because as far as we can see – as far as our senses can detect – there is no hope for improvement. We can endure the physical and emotional hardships of this life only when our faith assures us there is something waiting that is worthy of our endurance.

Sin is a touchy subject, but it is not complicated, nor is it the guilt-ridden calamity we have allowed it to become. Sin is a natural tendency for all of us. Sin is separation – separation from God and separation from each other. When we sin against another, we do or say something that creates division between us.

Repentance, on the other hand, means to *turn around*, or to change direction. Repentance bridges the separation created by our sin. Apologies are a form of repentance. That is why repentance is a necessary part of receiving forgiveness and an important component to experiencing heaven on earth.

An experience of heaven on earth is not compatible with division or separation. Hell, on the other hand, is the very experience of being set apart. We do not feel we belong, no one understands us; no one really cares about or appreciates us. Hell on earth is suffering, loneliness, illness, and despair. When we do not recognize that we were created connected to God and to each other, that our true nature is one of being in relationship, then we live in opposition to our core being – and we are miserable. And we are too often willing to share that misery with others (and we wonder why they don't invite us over more often).

So, here is the point I missed: we are co-creators with God of our earthly experience. We can experience heaven, or we can experience hell. At times in our lives, we will experience both, but neither are permanent, eternal states, at least not as we understand them. God does not sentence us for eternity to either. We can, however, exercise some control over which state we experience most often. It does require faith, of course, especially in difficult times. It does require an understanding of sin and the actions we choose that drive a wedge between us and others, including God. Finally, it requires repentance – a willingness to admit our shortcomings and do whatever we need to do to bring ourselves back into fellowship with God and those around us. As we get better at maintaining relationships, we become increasingly aware of the nearness of the kingdom of heaven. And we don't even have to die to experience it!

For whatever reason, I missed that. But understanding eternal matters is not an intellectual exercise. Our intellects are not eternal. We must learn to view our lives through the eyes of faith if we wish to understand the mysteries of heaven and hell. Our ability to see by faith has no more to do with our IQ than our 100-yard dash time has to do with our ability to cook a perfect omelet.

Jesus did not worry about whether he was going to heaven or hell after he died -- he knew he would be with God -- and we should know that, too. Jesus knew there was no state of earthly misery that could separate him from the love of the Father -- and so should we. He knew that the beatings and crucifixion would hurt, just as our illnesses and betrayals hurt – and he knew they would pass – and we would do well to remember that, too.

The kingdom of heaven is at hand -- here and now. We can know it as a day-by-day and moment-by-moment state of being. It is reached through faith in our oneness with God. I do not know how I ever missed it.

Let us pray:

Loving and eternal God, you are faithful beyond our ability to imagine. You give us grace

upon grace upon grace, even when we choose to turn that grace into a hell on earth. Help us look to you in faith through our hardships, and in gratitude through our triumphs. It is there we will meet you in your kingdom, even here on earth. Amen.

Endnotes

1   Martin Luther King, Jr.,
http://www.drmartinlutherkingjr.com/mlkqu
otes.htm, accessed March 11, 2017.

2   St. Francis of Assisi,
http://www.nationalreview.com/corner/3429
53/preach-gospel-always-if-necessary-use-
words-stephen-p-white, accessed April 22,
2017.

3   William Whorton,
http://www.selfhelpdaily.com/quotes-about-
finding-faults-with-others/, accessed March
12, 2017.

4   Mother Teresa of Calcutta,
http://www.goodreads.com/quotes/2887-if-
you-judge-people-you-have-no-time-to-love,
accessed March 12, 2017.

5   Fr. Richard Rohr,
http://www.azquotes.com/quote/730572,
accessed March 12, 2017.

6   Pierre Khawand, http://www.people-
onthego.com/blog/bid/57984/When-
everything-is-a-priority-nothing-is-a-priority-
Overcome-priority-overload, accessed March
19, 2017.

7   Richard Rohr, <u>Yes, And…</u>, Franciscan Media,
Cincinnati, OH. 2013, page 391.

8   Gretchen Rubin,
     http://www.goodreads.com/quotes/239043-
     the-days-are-long-but-the-years-are-short,
     accessed March 24, 2017.

9   Sr. Audrey Doetzel, *The 21ˢᵗ Century Need for
     Mystics and Prophets,* workshop given in Kansas
     City, MO on November 12, 2016.

10   Bob Dylan, http://www.metrolyrics.com/the-
     times-they-are-achangin-lyrics-bob-dylan.html,
     accessed April 22, 2017.

11   Paul Simon, http://www.metrolyrics.com/the-
     sound-of-silence-lyrics-simon-and-
     garfunkel.html, accessed April 22, 2017.

12   Paul Kalanithi, <u>When Breath Becomes Air</u>,
     Random House, New York. 2016, page 171.

13   Robert Greenleaf, *The Servant as Leader,*
     Greenleaf Institute. 1970.

14   Richard Rohr, <u>A Spring Within Us</u>, CAC
     Publishing, Albuquerque, NM. 2016.

All Biblical references are from the New Revised Standard Version (NRSV) translation.

ABOUT THE AUTHOR

Greg Hildenbrand lives south of Lawrence, Kansas with his wife, Carrie. They have two adult children, Grace and Reid. Greg is a volunteer leader of blended worship at First United Methodist Church in Lawrence and is the executive director for *Life Star of Kansas*. Greg's weekly blog, *Life Notes*, along with a number of his songs and other information is available from his website, www.ContemplatingGrace.com.

Greg Hildenbrand

Made in the USA
Middletown, DE
01 May 2017